Can you break the
CODE?

CODE BREAKER

USE THE CODES BELOW TO HELP ANSWER THE
CODE BREAKER QUESTIONS WITHIN THE WORKBOOK

CONTENTS

1 | Allah loves kindness.. 06
2 | Allah loves those who excel 11
3 | The Prophet ﷺ loved Aisha رضي الله عنها 14
4 | The Quran will soften your heart...................... 17
5 | Ask Allah for Jannatul Firdaws.......................... 20
6 | Allah loves the patient 23
7 | Allah loves beauty 26
8 | Being the best to your family............................ 29
9 | Remember Allah & He will remember you 32
10 | Loving the Prophet ﷺ 37
11 | Giving gifts increases love 40
12 | Allah loves those who love to meet Him........ 43
13 | The best of you has the best manners 46
14 | The best of you spreads salaam first.............. 49
15 | If you ask, ask from Allah 52
16 | Allah loves those who frequently repent 55
17 | The Prophet ﷺ began with his right side 58
18 | Allah loves Mecca 61
19 | A good word is charity 64
20 | Jibreel's عليه السلام wings................................. 69
21 | Khadijah رضي الله عنها promised paradise 72
22 | Abu Bakr رضي الله عنه the closest to the Prophet ﷺ 75
23 | Having your dua answered 78
24 | Allah loves generosity 81
25 | Don't be sad, Allah is with us............................ 84
26 | Good deeds erase bad deeds 87
27 | Dua that is answered on Fridays 90
28 | Revelation of the Quran 93
29 | Barakah in your family.. 96
30 | Allah loves those who trust Him....................... 99
31 | Allah answering our duas 104
32 | Allah loves those who purify themselves 107
33 | Allah loves deeds that are continuous............ 110
34 | Allah loves those who are just 113
35 | Ayatul Kursi as protection................................. 116

Reward Chart

Dearest viewers, welcome to your new workbook!

There are 35 worksheets to complete, you can find the answers for the worksheets based on every episode of The Azharis. Each worksheet will help you learn more about Allah.

Once you have completed the worksheet choose the matching sticker from the sticker page and stick it in correctly after each episode or if you prefer colour it in.

Episode 1

Episode 2

Episode 3

Episode 4

Episode 5

Episode 6

Episode 7

Episode 8

Episode 9

Episode 10

Episode 11

Episode 12

Episode 13

Episode 14

Episode 15

DON'T FORGET!

On completion of episodes 10, 20 & 30
you are able to download your
achievement certificates from
www.theazharis.com

Episode 16

Episode 17

Episode 18

Episode 19

Episode 20

Episode 21

Episode 22

Episode 23

Episode 24

Episode 25

Episode 26

Episode 27

Episode 28

Episode 29

Episode 30

Episode 31

Episode 32

Episode 33

Episode 34

Episode 35

Allah loves kindness

EPISODE - 1

1- What was the name of the Angel in the story of Taif?

Break the code | Refer to the code breaker sheet

_ _ _ _ _ _ _

2- Which shoe is Sunnah to put on first?

Find your way to the correct answer

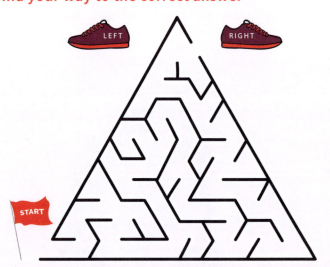

3- What is the Dua after Wudu?

Colour in

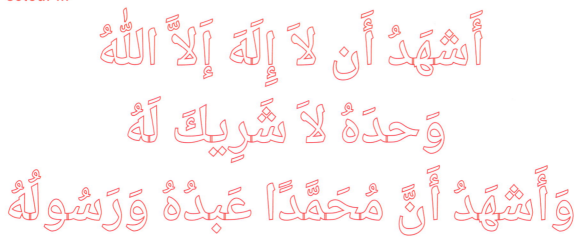

Ash-hadu an laa ilaaha illallaahu wahdahu laa shareeka lahu,
wa ash-hadu anna Muhammadan 'abduhu wa Rasooluhu

[Muslim]

REMEMBER THE REWARD
★ YOU CAN CHOOSE WHICH GATE OF JANNAH YOU ENTER FROM!

[Tirmidhi]

4- Which animal did not move when asked to by Abraha?

Join the dots and write the answer

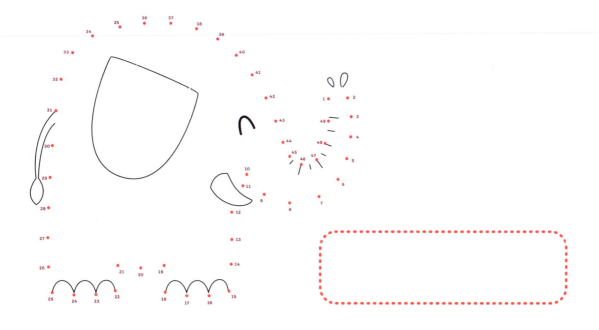

5- Which Prophet's people asked for cucumbers?

Circle the correct answer and colour the cucumber

Musa
عليه السلام

Eesa
عليه السلام

Ibrahim
عليه السلام

6- Which Prophet was thrown into the well?

Trace the letters YUSUF
عليه السلام

COMPETITION TIME!

A N S W E R S CIRCLE THE CORRECT ANSWER		S C O R E
1.	Two	Four	
2.	Ayatul Kursi	Surah Al Baqarah	
3.	Left	Right	
T O T A L S C O R E		**/6**

Watch **EPISODE 1** for the questions and circle the correct answer
Each correct answer is worth 2 points, leaving you with a total score out of 6.

LET'S SEE IF YOU CAN BEAT
THE AZHARIS

THE AZHARIS GAME CARDS

THE AZHARIS GAME CARDS

Kind
ALLAH LOVES

Wudu
WORSHIP

Cucumber
HEALTH

Well
PROPHETIC STORIES

Right Foot
CHARACTER / SUNNAH

Elephant
QUR'AN

Allah loves those who excel

EPISODE - 2

1- Which animal in the Qur'an was mentioned in this episode?

Join the dots and write the answer

2- Which Prophet was sent a camel as a sign?

Trace the letters

SALIH عليه السلام

3- Which month are the gates to Jannah open?

Break the code | Refer to the code breaker sheet

___ ___ ___ ___ ___ ___ ___

4- Allah loves those who _____

Complete the sentence

5- Wordsearch

Tick off the words as you find them

J	S	A	L	L	A	H
A	B	A	Q	O	P	E
N	G	R	L	G	D	X
N	S	O	F	I	V	M
A	J	H	O	U	H	L
H	Y	N	T	D	C	W
I	Z	L	I	O	N	K

☆ Allah

☆ Jannah

☆ Salih

☆ Good

☆ Lion

6- What type of heart should we have?

Colour the correct answer

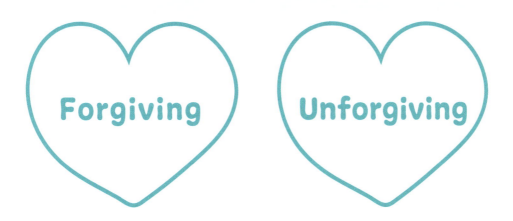

Forgiving

Unforgiving

COMPETITION TIME!

A N S W E R S CIRCLE THE CORRECT ANSWER		S C O R E
1.	Surah Yaseen	Surah Al Kahf	
2.	Camel	Snake	
3.	Battle of Badr	Battle of Uhud	
T O T A L S C O R E		/6

Watch **EPISODE 2** for the questions and circle the correct answer
Each correct answer is worth 2 points, leaving you with a total score out of 6.

LET'S SEE IF YOU CAN BEAT
THE AZHARIS

The Prophet ﷺ loved Aisha
رضي اللّه عنها

EPISODE - 3

1- Who was most beloved to the Prophet ﷺ?

Colour in

Aisha رضي اللّه عنها

2- What language is the Qur'an in?

Follow the maze to the correct answer

Arabic

English

3- Who discovered Zam Zam?

Break the code | Refer to the code breaker sheet

____ ____ ____ ____ ____

4- Which act wipes out all your sins?

Write the correct answer and colour the picture

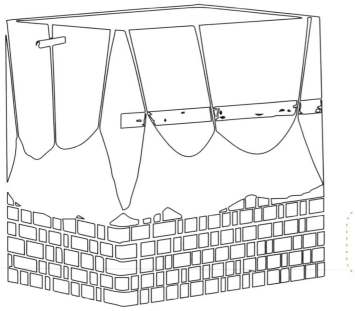 

5- What should you recite before bed to be protected?

Trace the letters

AYATUL KURSI

6- Which exercise was mentioned in this episode?

Circle the right picture

Sit Up

Forward Roll

Star Jump

COMPETITION TIME!

ANSWERS CIRCLE THE CORRECT ANSWER		SCORE
1.	Right Side	On your back	
2.	100 wings	600 wings	
3.	Friday	Monday	
TOTAL SCORE		**/6**

Watch **EPISODE 3** for the questions and circle the correct answer
Each correct answer is worth 2 points, leaving you with a total score out of 6.

LET'S SEE IF YOU CAN BEAT
THE AZHARIS

The Qur'an will soften your heart

EPISODE - 4

1- Dua between the Adhan and Iqamah is accepted?

Colour the correct answer

TRUE - FALSE

2- Your previous sins will be forgiven if you...

Find your way to the correct answer

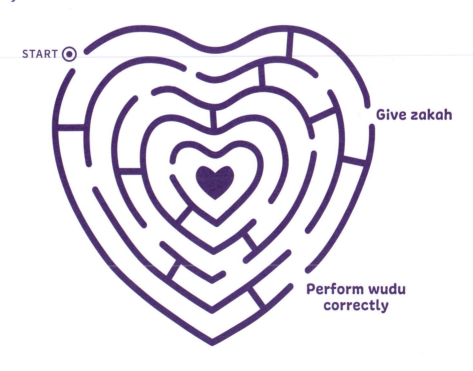

START

Give zakah

Perform wudu correctly

3- What can help soften our hearts?

Break the code | Refer to the code breaker sheet

_ _ _ _   _ _ _ _ _ _ _ _

4- What day should we recite Surah Al Kahf?

Circle the correct answer

5- What hand do we eat with?

Write the answer | Colour the correct hand

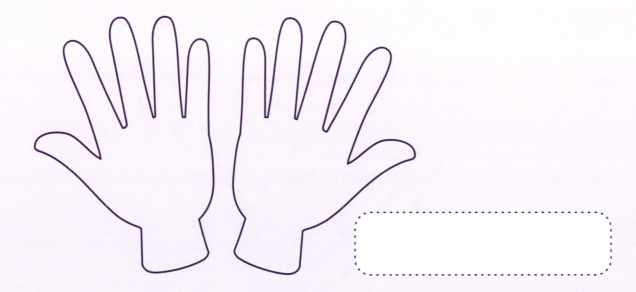

6- What did Prophet Musa عليه السلام say when asked what he uses his staff for?

Write your answer below

_____

_____

_____

COMPETITION TIME!

ANSWERS		SCORE
CIRCLE THE CORRECT ANSWER		
1. Yusuf عليه السلام	Yaqub عليه السلام	
2. Harun عليه السلام	Haman	
3. Audhubillah	Bismillah	
TOTAL SCORE		**/6**

Watch **EPISODE 4** for the questions and circle the correct answer
Each correct answer is worth 2 points, leaving you with a total score out of 6.

LET'S SEE IF YOU CAN BEAT
THE AZHARIS

Ask Allah for Jannatul Firdaws

EPISODE - 5

1- In which battle was the Prophet's ﷺ tooth broken?

Write your answer | Colour the picture

2- The Prophet ﷺ was accused of being a:

Break the code | Refer to the code breaker sheet

___ ___ ___ ___

3- What happens when Muslims shake hands?

Write the answer

_____

_____

_____

4- Paradise lies beneath the feet of

Colour the correct answer

Mother

Father

5- The Prophet ﷺ liked to eat _____

Unscamble the letters

N O Y H E

6- When we make dua for Jannah we should ask for?

Trace the letters

FIRDAWS

[BEST PLACE IN JANNAH]

COMPETITION TIME!

ANSWERS		SCORE
CIRCLE THE CORRECT ANSWER		
1.	**Musa** عليه السلام	**Dawud** عليه السلام	
2.	**Khadijah** رضي الله عنها	**Aisha** رضي الله عنها	
3.	**Abu Bakr** رضي الله عنه	**Bilal** رضي الله عنه	
TOTAL SCORE		/6

Watch EPISODE 5 for the questions and circle the correct answer
Each correct answer is worth 2 points, leaving you with a total score out of 6.

LET'S SEE IF YOU CAN BEAT

THE AZHARIS

Allah loves the patient

EPISODE - 6

1- Allah loves people who are:

Break the code | Refer to the code breaker sheet

___ ___ ___ ___ ___ ___ ___ ___

2- The Dua for rain is:

Colour in

Allahumma Sayyiban Naafian

[Bukhari]

3- Which animal was said to have eaten Prophet Yusuf عليه السلام?

Join the dot to dot and write the answer

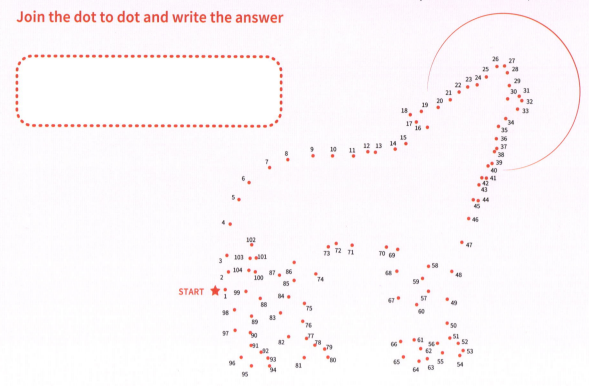

4- How many Angels make dua for you if you visit a sick person?

Tick the correct answer

☐ **50,000**   ☐ **60,000**   ☐ **70,000**

5- What is the name of the green dinosaur in The Azharis?

Write the answer below

6- Wordsearch

Tick off the words as you find them

☆ Allah

☆ Yusuf

☆ Rain

☆ Dua

☆ Wolf

J	S	A	L	L	A	H
A	Y	A	Q	O	P	E
N	U	R	W	G	D	X
N	S	O	F	O	V	M
D	U	A	O	U	L	L
H	F	Z	T	D	C	F
I	R	A	I	N	N	K

COMPETITION TIME!

ANSWERS CIRCLE THE CORRECT ANSWER		SCORE
1. Hawaa	Hajar	
2. Mecca	Medinah	
3. Hajar	Huda	
TOTAL SCORE		/6

Watch **EPISODE 6** for the questions and circle the correct answer
Each correct answer is worth 2 points, leaving you with a total score out of 6.

LET'S SEE IF YOU CAN BEAT
THE AZHARIS

Allah loves beauty

EPISODE - 7

1- What will the clothes be made of in Jannah?

Trace the correct word

Cotton OR Silk

2- What will be the first food in Jannah?

Join the dots and write the answer

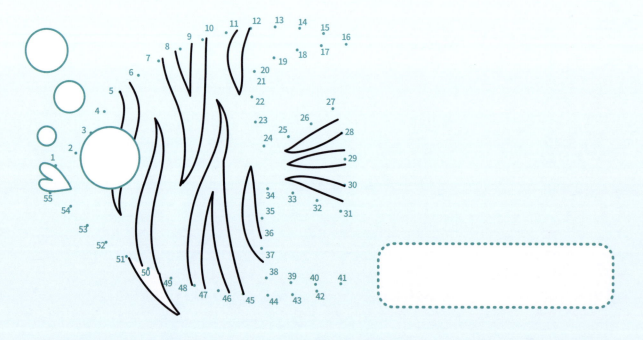

3- Who was made to sleep for 100 years?

Break the code | Refer to the code breaker sheet

___ ___ ___ ___ ___ ___ ___

___ ___ ___ ___ ___

4- For every step towards the masjid you get a good deed?

Colour the correct answer

5- Allah loves beauty.

Draw something you find beautiful

6- Telling the truth will lead you to:

Colour in

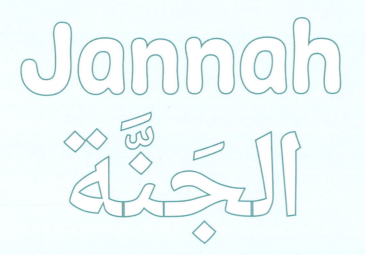

Jannah
الْجَنَّةُ

COMPETITION TIME!

ANSWERS CIRCLE THE CORRECT ANSWER			SCORE
1.	Monday	Saturday	
2.	Softly	Harshly	
3.	Green	Yellow	
TOTAL SCORE			**/6**

Watch **EPISODE 7** for the questions and circle the correct answer
Each correct answer is worth 2 points, leaving you with a total score out of 6.

LET'S SEE IF YOU CAN BEAT
THE AZHARIS

Being the best to your family

EPISODE - 8

1- What did the Prophet Nuh عليه السلام build?

Write the answer and colour the picture

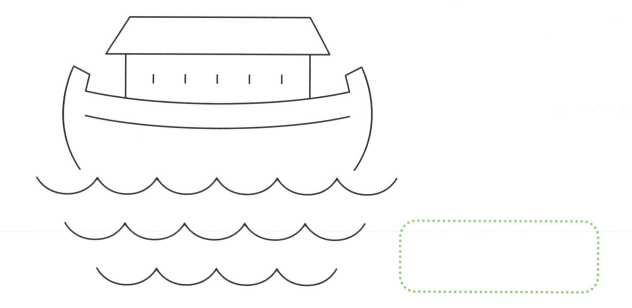

2- A grey hair will be a light on the day of judgement?

Circle the correct answer

TRUE - FALSE

3- Give an example of how we can be good to our family?

Write the answer below

_____

_____

_____

4- If you are merciful to others, Allah will be:

Underline the correct answer

Angry with you   -   Merciful to you   -   Happy with you

5- Wordsearch

Tick off the words as you find them

S	M	A	L	I	A	H
Y	B	E	W	U	D	U
R	N	L	R	E	D	K
I	O	U	F	C	L	E
A	J	V	H	U	Y	L
H	Y	E	E	D	C	W
I	Z	L	H	A	R	K

☆ Nuh

☆ Ark

☆ Hair

☆ Mercy

☆ Wudu

6- How many times do you wipe your head in wudu?

Circle the correct answer

ONE   FIVE   SEVEN

COMPETITION TIME!

ANSWERS CIRCLE THE CORRECT ANSWER			**SCORE**
1.	White	Grey	
2.	70	70,000	
3.	Surah Al Fatiha	Surah Al Alaq	
TOTAL SCORE			**/6**

Watch **EPISODE 8** for the questions and circle the correct answer
Each correct answer is worth 2 points, leaving you with a total score out of 6.

LET'S SEE IF YOU CAN BEAT
THE AZHARIS

Remember Allah & He will remember you

EPISODE - 9

1- Which flying insect was mentioned in this episode?

Break the code | Refer to the code breaker sheet

___ ___ ___ ___ ___ ___ ___ ___

2- What is the name of the angel that will blow the trumpet?

Colour the correct answer

Jibril
عليه السلام

Israfil
عليه السلام

Mikail
عليه السلام

3- Not thanking people means not thanking:

Trace the letters

4- If you remember Allah, he will:

Underline the correct answer

Remember you   -   Forget you   -   Abandon you

5- When eating we should eat from which part of the plate?

Find your way to the answer

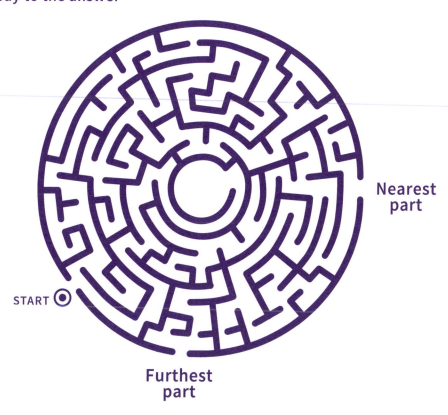

Nearest part

START ◎

Furthest part

6- Which animal was mentioned to have been sent to Firawn?

Join the dots and write the answer

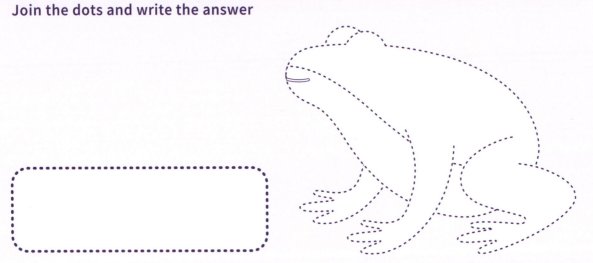

COMPETITION TIME!

ANSWERS CIRCLE THE CORRECT ANSWER		SCORE
1.	Right	Left	
2.	Bilal رضي الله عنه	Abu Bakr رضي الله عنه	
3.	Surah Al Baqarah	Surah Al Imran	
TOTAL SCORE		**/6**

Watch EPISODE 9 for the questions and circle the correct answer
Each correct answer is worth 2 points, leaving you with a total score out of 6.

LET'S SEE IF YOU CAN BEAT
THE AZHARIS

THE AZHARIS GAME CARDS

THE AZHARIS GAME CARDS

To Love
ALLAH LOVES

Hear
HEREAFTER

Together
HEALTH

Put
PROPHETIC STORIES

Neighbour
CHARACTER / SUNNAH

To Order
QUR'AN

Loving the Prophet ﷺ

EPISODE - 10

1- We should eat _____ with our families.

Find your way to the correct answer

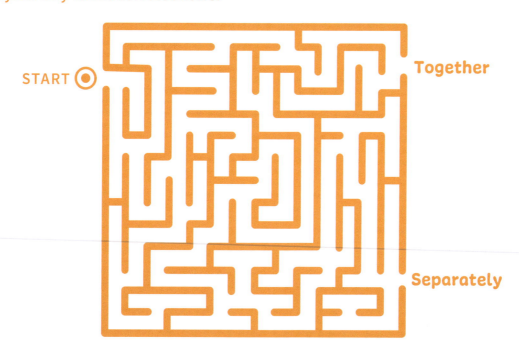

START

Together

Separately

2- What did the people of Nuh عليه السلام put their fingers in?

Trace the correct answer

Ears - Nose

3- What would you like in Jannah?

Write the answer

_____

_____

_____

4- When we advise people we should be the:

Tick the correct answer

⬡ first person to do it

⬡ last person to do it

⬡ person to never do it

5- Wordsearch

Tick off the words as you find them

J	E	A	R	I	A	J
A	B	S	W	H	N	A
L	G	L	U	E	D	N
L	O	N	F	I	L	N
A	J	V	O	X	H	A
H	Y	E	A	T	C	H
I	Z	L	N	A	T	E

☆ Allah

☆ Ear

☆ Nuh

☆ Jannah

☆ Eat

6- If you love Allah, He will

Trace the words

COMPETITION TIME!

A N S W E R S		SCORE
CIRCLE THE CORRECT ANSWER		
1. **Musa** عليه السلام	**Eesa** عليه السلام	
2. **Nuh** عليه السلام	**Adam** عليه السلام	
3. Surah Al Fatiha	Surah An Nas	
TOTAL SCORE		**/6**

Watch EPISODE 10 for the questions and circle the correct answer
Each correct answer is worth 2 points, leaving you with a total score out of 6.

LET'S SEE IF YOU CAN BEAT
THE AZHARIS

Giving gifts increases love

EPISODE - 11

1- What is the name of a river in Jannah?

Break the code | Refer to the code breaker sheet

____ ____ ____ ____ ____ ____ ____

2- Who did Musa عليه السلام go to in this episode?

Write your answer below

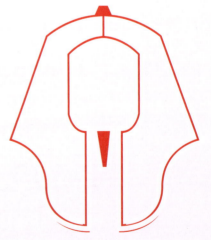

3- Which animal was eating the bread in the story?

Colour the picture and write the answer

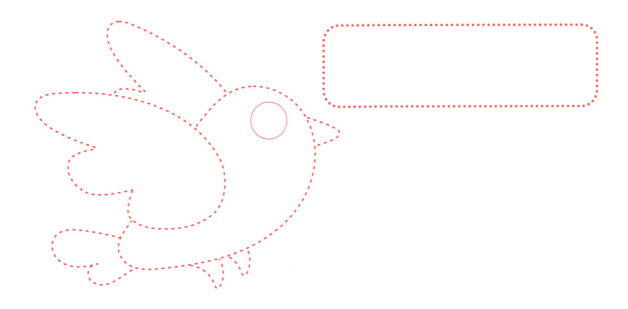

4- When you give gifts you will:

Trace the words

Love each other

5- Your friends are a reflection of your?

Tick the correct answer

☐ **Iman**

☐ **Qur'an**

☐ **Hadith**

6- What do you say when you sneeze?

Colour and trace the letters

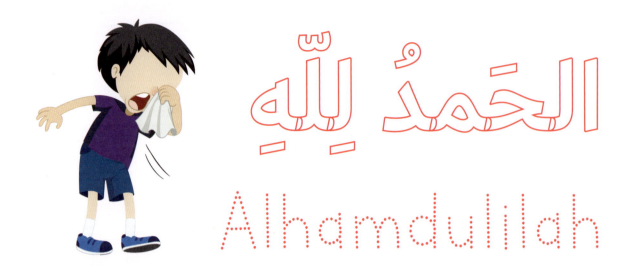

الْحَمْدُ لِلّٰه

Alhamdulilah

COMPETITION TIME!

ANSWERS CIRCLE THE CORRECT ANSWER		SCORE
1.	Surah Al Fatiha	Ayatul Kursi	
2.	40 years old	63 years old	
3.	Mecca	Medinah	
TOTAL SCORE		**/6**

Watch EPISODE 11 for the questions and circle the correct answer
Each correct answer is worth 2 points, leaving you with a total score out of 6.

LET'S SEE IF YOU CAN BEAT
THE AZHARIS

Allah loves those who love to meet Him

EPISODE - 12

1- Who knows the unseen?

Colour in and write the answer

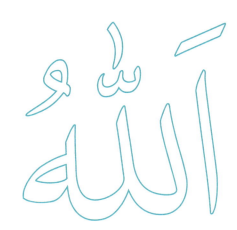

أَللّٰه

2- Which fruit was mentioned in the story of Yusuf عليه السلام?

Spell it out

P a P e l

3- What is the name of The Azharis nasheed?

Break the code | Refer to the code breaker sheet

____ ____ ____ ____ ____

____ ____ ____ ____ ____

____ ____ ____ ____

4- If you love to meet Allah, He will

Trace the words

5- Which animal are Muslims not allowed to eat?

Write the answer

6- Write the names of the people who are close to you.

○ ——————————

○ ——————————

○ ——————————

○ ——————————

COMPETITION TIME!

ANSWERS CIRCLE THE CORRECT ANSWER		SCORE
1.	Yusuf عليه السلام	Yaqub عليه السلام	
2.	Surah Al Ikhlas	Surah Al Kawthar	
3.	Musa عليه السلام	Eesa عليه السلام	
TOTAL SCORE		/6

Watch EPISODE 12 for the questions and circle the correct answer
Each correct answer is worth 2 points, leaving you with a total score out of 6.

LET'S SEE IF YOU CAN BEAT
THE AZHARIS

The best of
you has the
best manners

EPISODE - 13

1- What day is Jummah?

Circle the correct answer

Thursday

Friday

Saturday

2- Write an example of good manners

_____

_____

_____

3- Should you remind others when you have helped them?

Choose the correct answer

Yes   -   No

4- What was Musa عليه السلام told to take off when he spoke to Allah?

Break the code | Refer to the code breaker sheet

___ ___ ___ ___ ___ ___ ___

5- The pleasure of Allah is in pleasing our?

Find your way to the correct answer

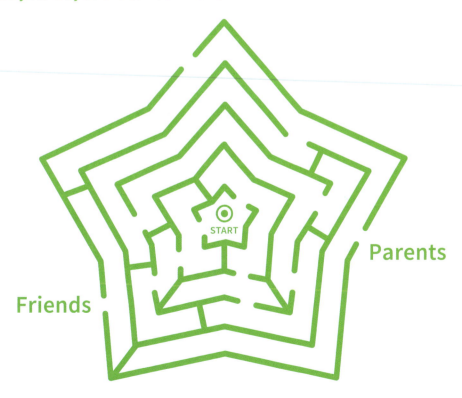

START

Parents

Friends

6- You plant a palm tree in Jannah by saying:

Colour in

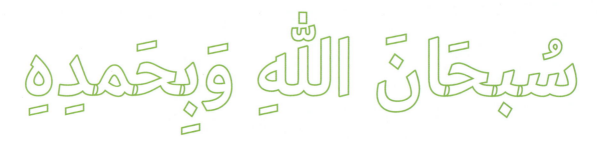

SubhanAllahi wa bi hamdihi
[Tirmidhi]

COMPETITION TIME!

ANSWERS CIRCLE THE CORRECT ANSWER		SCORE
1.	Ka'bah	Masjid Al Aqsa	
2.	Nuh عليه السلام	Idris عليه السلام	
3.	Idris عليه السلام	Harun عليه السلام	
TOTAL SCORE		**/6**

Watch **EPISODE 13** for the questions and circle the correct answer
Each correct answer is worth 2 points, leaving you with a total score out of 6.

LET'S SEE IF YOU CAN BEAT
THE AZHARIS

The best of you spreads salaam first

EPISODE - 14

1- What happens on the day of judgement?

Write your answer

_____

_____

_____

_____

_____

2- If we want more things, what should we do?

Trace the words

Be grateful

3- The best people to Allah are those who

Write the answer and colour in

_____

_____

_____

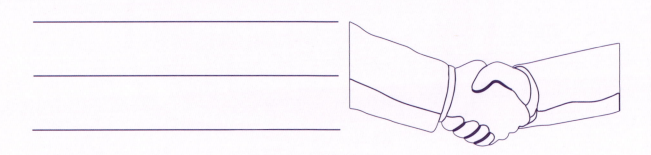

4- Your character is a reflection of your heart.

Circle the correct answer

TRUE | FALSE

5- Word Puzzle

Colour in the stars as you write the words in the boxes

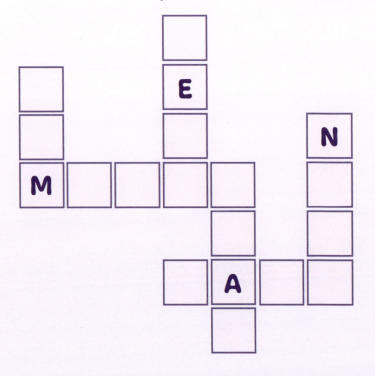

☆ Feet

☆ Nose

☆ Arm

☆ Mouth

☆ Face

☆ Head

6- Purity as part of your faith is:

Circle the correct answer

$\dfrac{1}{2}$

Half

$\dfrac{1}{3}$

Third

$\dfrac{1}{4}$

Quarter

COMPETITION TIME!

ANSWERS CIRCLE THE CORRECT ANSWER		SCORE
1.	Right	Left	
2.	Ibrahim عليه السلام	Eesa عليه السلام	
3.	Dates	Bread	
TOTAL SCORE		/6

Watch **EPISODE 14** for the questions and circle the correct answer
Each correct answer is worth 2 points, leaving you with a total score out of 6.

LET'S SEE IF YOU CAN BEAT
THE AZHARIS

If you ask, ask from Allah

EPISODE - 15

1- What is the name of the red Azhari dinosaur?

Write the answer below

2- For every sajdah you get raised how many ranks in Jannah?

Circle the correct answer

0
Zero

1
One

2
Two

3- Write something you make dua for

_____

_____

_____

_____

4- Where are the angels that write down our deeds?

Find your way to the answer

Shoulders

START ⦿

5- Where was the first Qiblah?

Trace the correct answer

Masjid Al Aqsa

Masjid An Nabawi

6- Wordsearch

Tick off the words as you find them

☆ Qiblah

☆ Angel

☆ Sajdah

☆ Jannah

☆ One

S	Q	A	R	O	A	J
A	A	I	W	N	N	A
L	N	J	B	E	D	N
L	O	G	D	L	L	N
A	J	V	E	A	A	A
H	Y	E	A	L	H	H
L	E	G	N	A	T	E

COMPETITION TIME!

ANSWERS		SCORE
CIRCLE THE CORRECT ANSWER		
1. Maghrib	Isha	
2. Before Fajr	Before Dhuhr	
3. Left	Right	
TOTAL SCORE		**/6**

Watch EPISODE 15 for the questions and circle the correct answer
Each correct answer is worth 2 points, leaving you with a total score out of 6.

LET'S SEE IF YOU CAN BEAT
THE AZHARIS

Allah loves those who repent frequently

EPISODE - 16

1- How much of our tummy should we fill when eating?

Circle the correct answer

$$\frac{1}{2}$$

Half

$$\frac{1}{3}$$

Third

$$\frac{1}{4}$$

Quarter

2- Where did the black stone come from?

Write the answer below

3- Allah sent messengers to people before us

Trace the correct answer

TRUE or FALSE

4- What do we say after praying?

Colour in

Astaghfirullah

[Muslim]

5- Allah loves those who _____

Join the dot to dot and write the answer

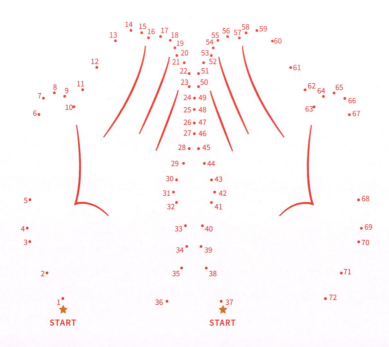

6- Which direction should we face when making dua?

Colour in and write the answer below

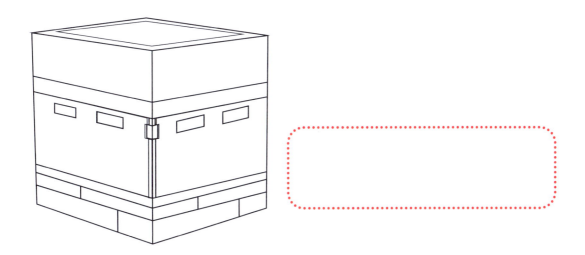

COMPETITION TIME!

ANSWERS			SCORE
	CIRCLE THE CORRECT ANSWER		
1.	Two	Four	
2.	63	83	
3.	One Third	Half	
TOTAL SCORE			/6

Watch **EPISODE 16** for the questions and circle the correct answer
Each correct answer is worth 2 points, leaving you with a total score out of 6.

LET'S SEE IF YOU CAN BEAT
THE AZHARIS

The Prophet ﷺ began with his right side

EPISODE - 17

1- Draw some of the signs of Allah in the sky

2- Where is the Prophet Muhammad's ﷺ mosque?

Colour the correct answer

Mecca   Medinah

Palestine

3- What is the main miracle Prophet Muhammad ﷺ came with?

Break the code | Refer to the code breaker sheet

___ ___ ___   ___ ___ ___ ___ ___

4- What side should you begin wudu with?

Circle the correct answer

Right - Left

5- What is the dua after wudu?

Trace the dua in Arabic

أَشْهَدُ أَنْ لَا إِلَهَ إِلَّا اللّٰهُ

وَحْدَهُ لَا شَرِيكَ لَهُ وَأَشْهَدُ

أَنَّ مُحَمَّدًا عَبْدُهُ وَرَسُولُهُ

6- What is the reward for the dua after wudu?

Underline the correct answer

★ Your past and future sins are forgiven

★ You can choose which gate of Jannah you want to enter in

★ You will be able to cross the sirat at the speed of lightening

COMPETITION TIME!

	A N S W E R S CIRCLE THE CORRECT ANSWER		**S C O R E**
1.	**Left**	**Right**	
2.	**Shuaib** عليه السلام	**Saleh** عليه السلام	
3.	**Two**	**Three**	
T O T A L S C O R E			**/6**

Watch **EPISODE 17** for the questions and circle the correct answer
Each correct answer is worth 2 points, leaving you with a total score out of 6.

LET'S SEE IF YOU CAN BEAT
THE AZHARIS

Allah loves Mecca

EPISODE - 18

1- If you forgive others, what will Allah do?

Write the answer below

_____

2- Where did Musa grow up?

Trace the picture and write the answer

3- Which Prophet was involved in the story of the cow?

Break the code | Refer to the code breaker sheet

____ ____ ____ ____

4- Which land is most beloved to Allah?

Colour in

5- About how many good deeds do we get for reciting Ayatul Kursi?

Circle the correct answer

500

700

1900

6- Wordsearch

Tick off the words as you find them

- ☆ Mecca
- ☆ Soft
- ☆ Musa
- ☆ Sister
- ☆ Cow

S	M	A	L	I	M	H
Y	I	E	W	U	U	U
W	N	S	C	E	S	K
I	O	U	T	C	A	E
A	J	C	H	E	A	L
H	Y	E	E	D	R	W
T	F	O	S	A	R	K

COMPETITION TIME!

ANSWERS CIRCLE THE CORRECT ANSWER		SCORE
1.	Mecca	Medinah	
2.	SubhanAllah	Alhamdulillah	
3.	Left	Right	
TOTAL SCORE		**/6**

Watch **EPISODE 18** for the questions and circle the correct answer
Each correct answer is worth 2 points, leaving you with a total score out of 6.

LET'S SEE IF YOU CAN BEAT
THE AZHARIS

A good word is charity

EPISODE - 19

1- How many angels write down our bad deeds?

Circle the correct answer

 1  3  4

2- If you know and live by 99 of Allah's names what happens?

Underline the correct answer

Live a life without trials | Be from the people of Jannah

3- How can we ask Allah for forgiveness?

Trace the letters

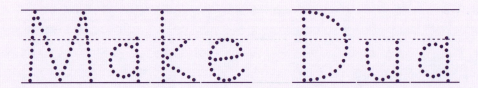

Make Dua

4- What is the dua the Prophet ﷺ made to be saved from Jahanum?

Colour in

Allahumma inni audhubika min adhabi jahanum
[Bukhari]

5- What was the name of the last series from the Azharis?

Break the code | Refer to the code breaker sheet

___ ___ ___   ___ ___   ___ ___ ___

___ ___ ___ ___ ___ ___ ___

6- Draw an example of giving charity

COMPETITION TIME!

ANSWERS CIRCLE THE CORRECT ANSWER		SCORE
1.	Yes	No	
2.	Dhuhr	Asr	
3.	From Dhuhr	From Fajr	
TOTAL SCORE		/6

Watch **EPISODE 19** for the questions and circle the correct answer
Each correct answer is worth 2 points, leaving you with a total score out of 6.

LET'S SEE IF YOU CAN BEAT
THE AZHARIS

THE AZHARIS GAME CARDS

Dad
FAMILY

Sleep
WORSHIP

Suhur
HEALTH

Jibril
PROPHETIC STORIES

Sunnah
CHARACTER / SUNNAH

Flood
QUR'AN

Jibreel's عليه السلام **wings**

EPISODE - 20

1- What punishment came to the people of Nuh عليه السلام ?

Break the code | Refer to the code breaker sheet

__ __ __ __ __ __

2- What do you eat for suhoor?

Draw and colour

3- Who sits down first?

Find your way to the correct answer

4- Which side should you sleep on?

Colour the correct answer

Right | Left

5- Feeding people is a _____

Unscamble the letters

N S N U H A

6- How many wings did Jibril عليه السلام have?

Circle the correct answer

400

600

500

COMPETITION TIME!

ANSWERS CIRCLE THE CORRECT ANSWER			SCORE
1.	Mecca	Masjid Al Aqsa	
2.	Aisha	Mariam	
3.	Two	Three	
TOTAL SCORE			/6

Watch EPISODE 20 for the questions and circle the correct answer
Each correct answer is worth 2 points, leaving you with a total score out of 6.

LET'S SEE IF YOU CAN BEAT
THE AZHARIS

1- Which shoe do you put on first?

Break the code | Refer to the code breaker sheet

____ ____ ____ ____ ____

2- What animal did the Prophets look after?

Colour in and write the answer

3- Angels are made out of fire?

Circle the correct answer

True - False

4- How can we respect the Quran?

Trace the words

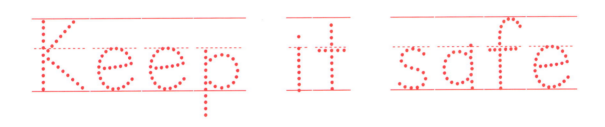

5- What should we break our fast with first of all?

Underline the correct answer

Toast

Dates

Rice

6- What was the name of the Prophet's ﷺ first wife?

Break the code | Refer to the code breaker sheet

___ ___ ___ ___ ___ ___ ___ ___

COMPETITION TIME!

ANSWERS		SCORE
CIRCLE THE CORRECT ANSWER		
1. **Yusuf** عليه السلام	**Musa** عليه السلام	
2. **Arabic**	**English**	
3. **Mikail** عليه السلام	**Jibril** عليه السلام	
TOTAL SCORE		**/6**

Watch **EPISODE 21** for the questions and circle the correct answer
Each correct answer is worth 2 points, leaving you with a total score out of 6.

LET'S SEE IF YOU CAN BEAT
THE AZHARIS

Abu Bakr the closest to the Prophet ﷺ

EPISODE - 22

1- Who was the Prophet Muhammad's ﷺ best friend?

Colour in

Abu Bakr

رضي الله عنه

2- What should you do when you hear the adhan?

Trace the words

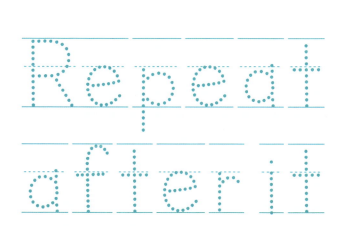

Repeat after it

3- Who keeps birds safe in the air?

Write the answer and colour the picture

4- What was the name of the person Musa عليه السلام was sent to?

Colour the correct answer

Haman - Firawn

5- What will run under your house in Jannah?

Find your way to the answer

START

Mountains

Rivers

6- Wordsearch

Tick off the words as you find them

☆ Adhan

☆ Bird

☆ Musa

☆ Jannah

☆ Allah

J	S	A	L	L	A	H
A	A	A	D	H	A	N
M	G	N	L	G	L	X
N	U	O	N	I	L	M
A	J	S	O	A	A	L
H	Y	N	A	D	H	W
B	I	R	D	O	N	K

COMPETITION TIME!

	ANSWERS CIRCLE THE CORRECT ANSWER		**SCORE**
1.	Allah forgives me	Allah hears everything	
2.	Two Rakats	Four Rakats	
3.	23 years	53 years	
TOTAL SCORE			**/6**

Watch **EPISODE 22** for the questions and circle the correct answer
Each correct answer is worth 2 points, leaving you with a total score out of 6.

LET'S SEE IF YOU CAN BEAT
THE AZHARIS

Having your dua answered

EPISODE - 23

1- What time of the day was mentioned that dua is accepted?

Choose the correct picture

Morning

Afternoon

Night

2- What did Prophet Sulaiman ask to be brought from Bilqis?

Circle the correct answer

Throne - Gifts

3- What surah makes Shaitan run away from your house?

Find your way to the answer

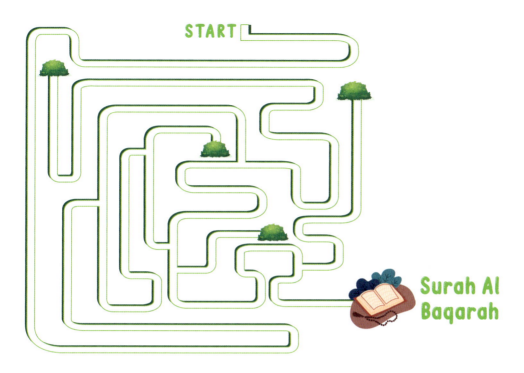

4- What was the name of the person who built the wall in the story?

Circle the correct answer

Khadijah   Khidr   Kawthar

5- Spending time with family will benefit you in this life and the akhirah?

Colour the correct answer

True or False

6- This is a treasure from Jannah:

Colour in

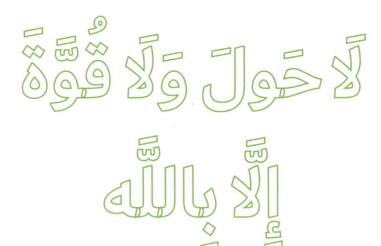

La hawla wa la quwatta ila billah

[Bukhari]

COMPETITION TIME!

ANSWERS CIRCLE THE CORRECT ANSWER		SCORE
1.	Hawaa / Hajar	
2.	Ismail عليه السلام / Ibrahim عليه السلام	
3.	Idris عليه السلام / Yusuf عليه السلام	
TOTAL SCORE		**/6**

Watch **EPISODE 23** for the questions and circle the correct answer
Each correct answer is worth 2 points, leaving you with a total score out of 6.

LET'S SEE IF YOU CAN BEAT
THE AZHARIS

Allah loves generosity

EPISODE - 24

1- What was mentioned as the rope to success in this life and the next?

Break the code | Refer to the code breaker sheet

__ __   __ __   __ __   __ __   __ __   __ __

2- Which Surah is equal to one third of the Quran?

Colour the correct answer

Surah Fatiha | Surah Ikhlas

3- Which row has most reward for men in prayer?

Put a tick next to the correct answer

1ˢᵀ ☐ | 2ᴺᴰ ☐

4- How will the bridge of Jahanum be?

Underline the correct answer

Soft - Wide - Sharp

5- What does it mean to backbite?

Trace the words

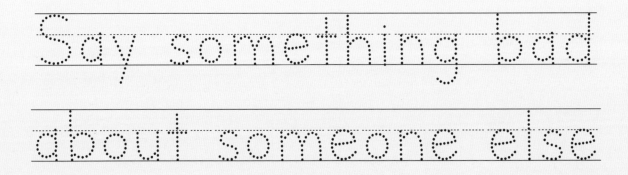

Say something bad
about someone else

6- Draw an example of how we can be generous?

COMPETITION TIME!

ANSWERS CIRCLE THE CORRECT ANSWER		SCORE
1.	Muharram	Ramadan	
2.	Zakah	Hajj	
3.	Give Charity	Read Quran	
TOTAL SCORE		/6

Watch **EPISODE 24** for the questions and circle the correct answer
Each correct answer is worth 2 points, leaving you with a total score out of 6.

LET'S SEE IF YOU CAN BEAT
THE AZHARIS

Don't be sad, Allah is with us

EPISODE - 25

1- Which prayer is better than everything else in the world?

Find your way to the correct answer

Isha Salah

Maghrib Salah

Asr Salah

Fajr Salah

START

2- If you give a fasting person food, you get the reward of:

Write the answer below

3- What should you do more of on Fridays?

Trace the answer

upon Prophet Muhammad ﷺ

4- What side is it Sunnah to start combing your hair from?

Tick the correct answer

⬡ **Middle**   ⬡ **Right**   ⬡ **Left**

5- Which mountain loves us?

Trace the picture and colour the correct answer

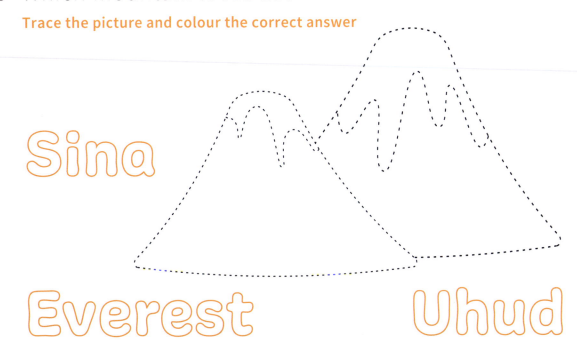

Sina

Everest

Uhud

6- When we feel sad, who will always be there to help us?

Write the answer and colour in

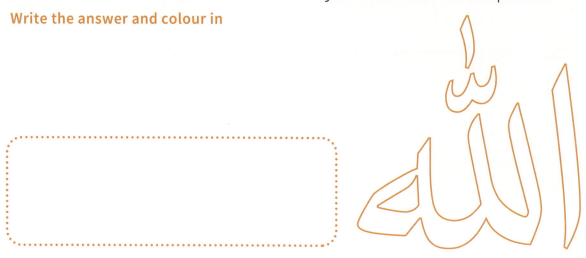

COMPETITION TIME!

ANSWERS		SCORE
CIRCLE THE CORRECT ANSWER		
1. Hajar	Huda	
2. Muhammad صلى الله عليه وسلّم	Eesa عليه السلام	
3. Mecca	Medinah	
TOTAL SCORE		**/6**

Watch **EPISODE 25** for the questions and circle the correct answer
Each correct answer is worth 2 points, leaving you with a total score out of 6.

LET'S SEE IF YOU CAN BEAT
THE AZHARIS

Good deeds erase bad deeds

EPISODE - 26

1- Which item of clothing did Prophet Yusuf's عليه السلام brothers bring back from the well?

Break the code | Refer to the code breaker sheet

—— — —— —— —— ——

2- Prophet Ibrahim عليه السلام was thrown into a fire.

Circle the correct answer

  **True   False**

3- When you do good deeds, what happens to your bad deeds?

Write the answer below

_____

_____

_____

_____

4- On the night of Isra wal Miraj the Prophet ﷺ went from:

Choose the correct answer and fill in the blanks

[ ]   to   [ ]

(Medinah - Mecca)   **(Mecca - Al Aqsa)**

5- What is the first prayer in the day?

Tick the correct answer

[ ] **Isha**

[ ] **Asr**

[ ] **Fajr**

6- Word Puzzle

Tick the words as you find them

☆ Mecca

☆ Yusuf

☆ Medinah

☆ Fire

☆ Shirt

☆ Fajr

COMPETITION TIME!

ANSWERS		SCORE
	CIRCLE THE CORRECT ANSWER	
1.	**Eesa** عليه السلام **Muhammad** صلى الله عليه وسلّم	
2.	**Eesa** عليه السلام **Yahya** عليه السلام	
3.	**Left** **Right**	
TOTAL SCORE		/6

Watch **EPISODE 26** for the questions and circle the correct answer
Each correct answer is worth 2 points, leaving you with a total score out of 6.

LET'S SEE IF YOU CAN BEAT
THE AZHARIS

Dua that is answered on Fridays

EPISODE - 27

1- Which Prophet was put in a basket as a baby?

Write the answer below

2- Which animal did Musa عليه السلام tell his people to sacrifice?

Trace the answer and colour in the animal

cow

3- What will be on the bracelets of people in Jannah?

Break the code | Refer to the code breaker sheet

____ ____ ____ ____   ____ ____ ____

____ ____ ____ ____ ____ ____

4- What did Allah call a lamp?

Colour the correct answer

Stars   **Moon**   **Sun**

5- Which day of the week has a specific time when dua is answered?

Circle the correct answer

Monday   **Tuesday**

Friday

6- Draw an example of how we can help others

COMPETITION TIME!

ANSWERS			SCORE
CIRCLE THE CORRECT ANSWER			
1.	Zakariyah عليه السلام	Eesa عليه السلام	
2.	Monday	Friday	
3.	Yaqub عليه السلام	Yusha عليه السلام	
TOTAL SCORE			**/6**

Watch EPISODE 27 for the questions and circle the correct answer
Each correct answer is worth 2 points, leaving you with a total score out of 6.

LET'S SEE IF YOU CAN BEAT
THE AZHARIS

Revelation of the Quran

EPISODE - 28

1- Spending time with your family is a good deed?

Circle the correct answer

TRUE

or

FALSE

2- Which animal did Allah send to show the sons of Adam how to bury someone?

Write the answer below

3- How do we perform wudu?

Number the parts in order

Hands   **Hair**   **Arms**   **Mouth**   **Feet**   **Face**   **Nose**

4- For approximately how long did the people of the cave sleep?

Find your way to the correct answer

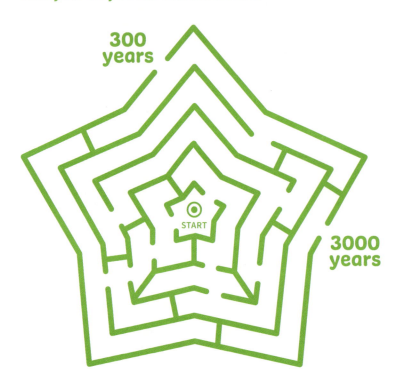

300 years

3000 years

START

5- What colour will the sun be on the day of judgement?

Colour the correct answer

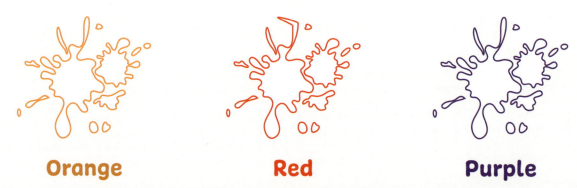

Orange   **Red**   **Purple**

6- When was the Quran sent down?

Break the code | Refer to the code breaker sheet

___ ___ ___ ___ ___ ___ ___ ___

___ ___ ___ ___

COMPETITION TIME!

ANSWERS CIRCLE THE CORRECT ANSWER		SCORE
1.	**Bilal** رضي الله عنه	**Umar** رضي الله عنه	
2.	Cats	Sheep	
3.	Monday	Friday	
TOTAL SCORE		**/6**

Watch **EPISODE 28** for the questions and circle the correct answer
Each correct answer is worth 2 points, leaving you with a total score out of 6.

LET'S SEE IF YOU CAN BEAT
THE AZHARIS

Barakah in your family

EPISODE - 29

1- Being good to your family brings barakah to your wealth?

Circle the correct answer

TRUE

FALSE

2- Allah says people will never be able to create which animal?

Trace the picture and write the answer

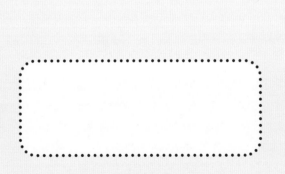

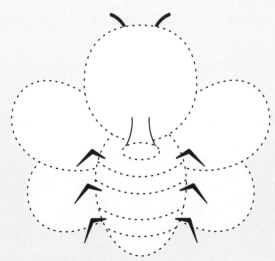

3- Word Puzzle

Tick the words as you find them

☆ Wudu

☆ Dua

☆ Wealth

☆ Fly

☆ Right

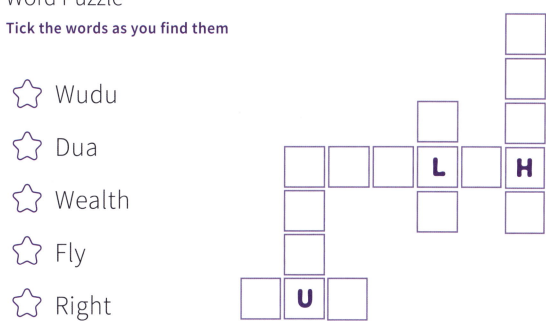

4- What hand do we eat with?

Colour the correct answer

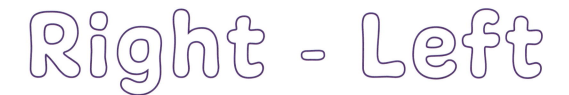

5- What was the name of the person that helped Firawn?

Break the code | Refer to the code breaker sheet

____ ____ ____ ____ ____

6- Which body part do you wash in wudu?

Tick the correct answer

○ **Knee**

○ **Feet**

○ **Hips**

COMPETITION TIME!

A N S W E R S CIRCLE THE CORRECT ANSWER		SCORE
1.	Abu Bakr رضي الله عنه	Musa عليه السلام	
2.	Dawud عليه السلام	Musa عليه السلام	
3.	Three	Four	
TOTAL SCORE		**/6**

Watch **EPISODE 29** for the questions and circle the correct answer
Each correct answer is worth 2 points, leaving you with a total score out of 6.

LET'S SEE IF YOU CAN BEAT
THE AZHARIS

Allah loves those who trust Him

EPISODE - 30

1- Which animal was mentioned in this episode?

Unscramble the letters and write the answer below

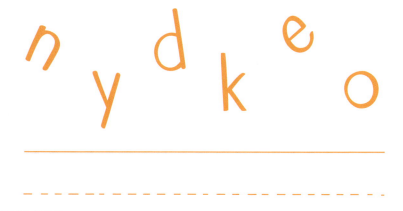

n y d k e o

_____

- - - - - - - - - - - - - - - - - - -

_____

2- What are the glasses in Jannah made from?

Break the code | Refer to the code breaker sheet

___ ___ ___ ___ ___ ___

3- Which insect was worried about being hurt by Prophet Sulaiman's عليه السلام army?

Find your way to the correct answer

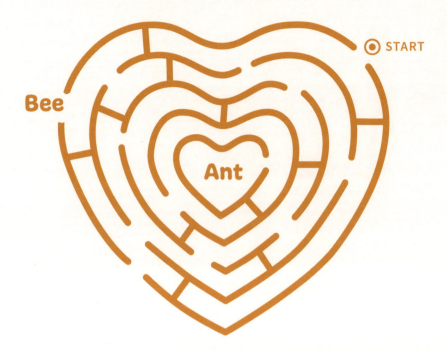

4- What do the fish do for someone that seeks knowledge?

Colour in

Makes dua for them

5- Allah says the successful people are those who concentrate when they pray

Trace the correct answer

 or

6- Allah loves those who:

Circle the correct answers

Are generous	**Are kind**	**Waste food**
Frequently repent	**Trust Him**	**Excel in good**
Argue with others	**Cheat and lie**	**Disobey parents**

COMPETITION TIME!

ANSWERS CIRCLE THE CORRECT ANSWER			SCORE
1.	Aisha رضي الله عنها	Khadijah رضي الله عنها	
2.	33 times	100 times	
3.	Israfil عليه السلام	Mikail عليه السلام	
TOTAL SCORE			**/6**

Watch EPISODE 30 for the questions and circle the correct answer
Each correct answer is worth 2 points, leaving you with a total score out of 6.

LET'S SEE IF YOU CAN BEAT
THE AZHARIS

Allah answering our duas

EPISODE - 31

1- Who did Allah send Prophet Musa عليه السلام to?

Colour in

Firawn

2- We will all be brought to life on the day of judgement?

Tick the correct answer

○ **True**

○ **False**

3- What happens when you help someone?

Write the answer

_____

_____

_____

4- How many times will the trumpet be blown at the end of time?

Circle the correct answer

 2    6    8

5- If you want to know your relationship with Allah, look at your relationship with the:

Find your way to the answer

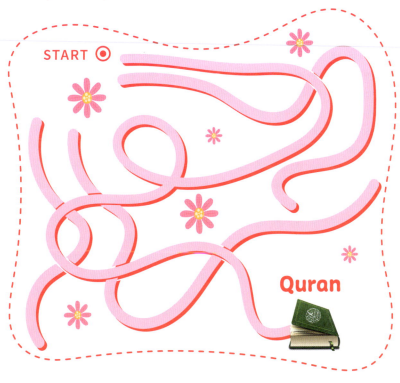

START

Quran

6- Allah loves those who:

Trace the words

COMPETITION TIME!

ANSWERS CIRCLE THE CORRECT ANSWER		SCORE
1.	Alhamdulillah	Bismillah	
2.	Cave Hira	Cave Thawr	
3.	Ramadan	Muharram	
TOTAL SCORE		**/6**

Watch EPISODE 31 for the questions and circle the correct answer
Each correct answer is worth 2 points, leaving you with a total score out of 6.

LET'S SEE IF YOU CAN BEAT

THE AZHARIS

THE AZHARIS GAME CARDS

THE AZHARIS GAME CARDS

Trust
ALLAH LOVES

Success
WORSHIP

Silver
HEREAFTER

Ant
PROPHETIC STORIES

Fish
CHARACTER / SUNNAH

Donkey
QUR'AN

Allah loves those who purify themselves

EPISODE - 32

1- Allah loves those who?

Colour in

Purify Themselves

2- Which person can control themselves when angry?

Break the code | Refer to the code breaker sheet

___ ___ ___ ___ ___ ___

3- The river of Al Kawthar is sweeter than:

Circle the correct answer

Chocolate

Honey

Sugar

4- Not a leaf falls except without Allah knowing?

Trace the correct answer

True - False

5- Word Puzzle

Tick the words as you find them

☆ Honey

☆ Quran

☆ Love

☆ Leaf

☆ Allah

☆ Anger

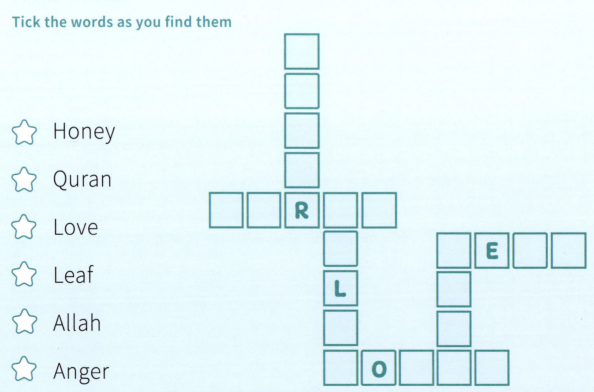

6- When saying we are going to do something we should say:

Colour in

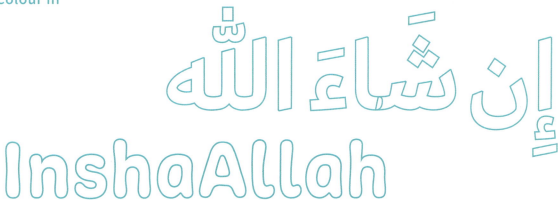

COMPETITION TIME!

A N S W E R S		SCORE
CIRCLE THE CORRECT ANSWER		
1. Abu Talib	Abdullah	
2. Jummah	Dhuhr	
3. Left Foot	Right Foot	
TOTAL SCORE		**/6**

Watch EPISODE 32 for the questions and circle the correct answer
Each correct answer is worth 2 points, leaving you with a total score out of 6.

LET'S SEE IF YOU CAN BEAT
THE AZHARIS

Allah loves deeds that are continuous

EPISODE - 33

1- If ink was used to write about Allah, what would happen to the ink?

Trace the words

It would run out

2- Wordsearch

Tick off the words as you find them

J	S	A	L	I	A	H
A	B	S	W	O	N	A
L	G	L	L	E	D	K
L	O	A	F	I	L	E
A	J	V	O	U	H	L
H	Y	E	E	D	C	W
I	Z	L	H	A	T	E

☆ Ink

☆ Slave

☆ Well

☆ Allah

☆ Love

☆ Hate

3- Should we hate others?

Trace the correct answer

YES | NO

4- The best of deeds are the ones done?

Colour the correct answer

Continuously
_____
Occasionally

5- Yusuf was sold as a slave for a small amount of money?

Circle the correct answer

True
or
False

6- Draw some fruits you want to eat in Jannah?

COMPETITION TIME!

A N S W E R S CIRCLE THE CORRECT ANSWER		SCORE
1.	Mecca	Medinah	
2.	Elephant	Rhino	
3.	Alhamdulillah	Bismillah	
TOTAL SCORE		**/6**

Watch **EPISODE 33** for the questions and circle the correct answer
Each correct answer is worth 2 points, leaving you with a total score out of 6.

LET'S SEE IF YOU CAN BEAT
THE AZHARIS

Allah loves those who are just

EPISODE - 34

1- A healthy body leads to a:

Break the code | Refer to the code breaker sheet

_____ _____ _____ _____ _____ _____ _____

_____ _____ _____ _____

2- Allah loves those who are:

Trace the word

3- Speak to others as you want to be spoken to

Circle the correct answer

True or False

4- When we become angry we should say:

Colour in

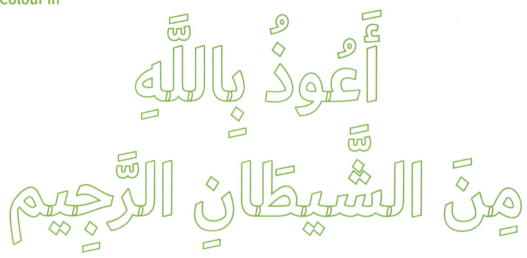

Audhubillahi min ashaytaanir rajeem

[Tirmidhi]

5- What will our good deeds be weighed on?

Circle the correct answer

Bag

Scale

Lift

6- Shaitan promises you: _____

Allah promises you: _____

Choose the correct word and fill in the blanks

Forgiveness | Poverty

COMPETITION TIME!

ANSWERS CIRCLE THE CORRECT ANSWER		SCORE
1.	Eesa عليه السلام	Muahmmad صلى الله عليه وسلّم	
2.	Amina	Khadijah رضي الله عنها	
3.	Two	Four	
TOTAL SCORE		**/6**

Watch EPISODE 34 for the questions and circle the correct answer
Each correct answer is worth 2 points, leaving you with a total score out of 6.

LET'S SEE IF YOU CAN BEAT
THE AZHARIS

Ayatul Kursi as protection

EPISODE - 35

1- Who ran between Mount Safa and Marwa?

Write the answer below

2- What is Istikarah?

Colour the correct answer

A Hadith   A verse in the Quran   A Prayer

3- What was the food mentioned that Musa's عليه السلام people wanted to eat?

Trace, colour and write the answer

4- What Surah should we recite before bed?

Circle the correct answer

Surah Al Layl   **3 Quls**   **Surah Al Fatiha**

5- Was Prophet Ibrahim's عليه السلام dua answered straight away?

Trace the correct answer

YES | NO

6- Which Prophet dreamt of , the ☀ and the 🌙?

Colour in

YUSUF

عليه السلام

COMPETITION TIME!

ANSWERS CIRCLE THE CORRECT ANSWER		SCORE
1.	**Yusuf** عليه السلام	**Eesa** عليه السلام	
2.	**Sulaiman** عليه السلام	**Dawud** عليه السلام	
3.	**Saleh** عليه السلام	**Eesa** عليه السلام	
TOTAL SCORE		**/6**

Watch EPISODE 35 for the questions and circle the correct answer
Each correct answer is worth 2 points, leaving you with a total score out of 6.

LET'S SEE IF YOU CAN BEAT

THE AZHARIS

Answers

EPISODE - 1

1- Jibreel

2- Right

3- ——

4- Elephant

5- Musa

6- ——

EPISODE - 2

1- Lion

2- ——

3- Ramadan

4- Excel in good

5- ——

6- Forgiving

EPISODE - 3

1- ——

2- Arabic

3- Hajar

4- Hajj

5- Ayatul Kursi

6- Sit up

EPISODE - 4

1- True

2- Perform wudu correctly

3- The Quran

4- Friday

5- Right Hand

6- Walking & Shepherding

EPISODE - 5

1- Uhud

2- Poet

3- Sins fall away like leaves fall off trees

4- Mother

5- Honey

6- Firdaws

EPISODE - 6

1- Patient

2- ——

3- Wolf

4- 70,000

5- Azhari Rex

6- ——

EPISODE - 7

1- Silk

2- Fish

3- Prophet Uzayr

4- True

5- ——

6- Jannah

EPISODE - 8

1- Ark

2- True

3- ——

4- Merciful to you

5- ——

6- One

EPISODE - 9

1- Mosquito

2- Israfil

3- Allah

4- Remember you

5- Nearest Part

6- Frog

EPISODE - 10

1- Together

2- Ears

3- ——

4- 1st person to do it

5- ——

6- Love You

EPISODE - 11

1- Kawthar

2- Firawn

3- Bird

4- Love each other

5- Iman

6- Alhamdulillah

EPISODE - 12

1- Allah

2- Apple

3- Rabbi Zidni Ilma

4- Love to meet you

5- Pig

6- ——

EPISODE - 13

1- Friday

2- ——

3- No

4- Sandals

5- Parents

6- ——

EPISODE - 14

1- We get our book of deeds

2- Be grateful

3- First to greet with salaam

4- True

5- ——

6- Half

EPISODE - 15

1- Azharisaurus

2- One

3- ——

4- Shoulders

5- Masjid Al Aqsa

6- ——

EPISODE - 16

1- One Third
2- Jannah
3- True
4- Astaghfirullah
5- Ask for forgiveness
6- Kabah

EPISODE - 17

1- Sun, Moon, Clouds
2- Medinah
3- The Quran
4- Right
5- ——
6- You can choose which gate of Jannah you want to enter in

EPISODE - 18

1- Forgive you
2- Palace
3- Musa
4- Mecca
5- 1500
6- ——

EPISODE - 19

1- One
2- Enter Jannah
3- Make Dua
4- ——
5- Juz by Juz Stories
6- ——

EPISODE - 20

1- Flood
2- ——
3- Dad
4- Right
5- Sunnah
6- 600

EPISODE - 21

1- Right
2- Sheep
3- False
4- Keep it Safe
5- Dates
6- Khadijah

EPISODE - 22

1- Abu Bakr
2- Repeat after it
3- Allah
4- Firawn
5- River
6- ——

EPISODE - 23

1- Night
2- Throne
3- Surah Al Baqarah
4- Khidr
5- True
6- ——

EPISODE - 24

1- Prayer
2- Surah Ikhlas
3- First
4- Sharp
5- Say something bad about someone else
6- ——

EPISODE - 25

1- Fajr Salah
2- Their Fast
3- Send Salaam
4- Right
5- Uhud
6- Allah

EPISODE - 26

1- Shirt
2- True
3- They get erased
4- Mecca to Medinah
5- Fajr
6- ——

EPISODE - 27

1- Musa
2- Cow
3- Gold and Pearls
4- Sun
5- Friday
6- ——

EPISODE - 28

1- True
2- Crow
3- Hands | Mouth | Nose | Face | Arms | Hair | Feet
4- 100 years
5- Red
6- Laylatul Qadr

EPISODE - 29

1- True
2- Fly
3- ——
4- Right
5- Haman
6- Feet

EPISODE - 30

1- Donkey
2- Silver
3- Ant
4- Makes dua for them
5- True
6- Are generous, Frequently repent, Are kind, Trust Him, Excel in good

EPISODE - 31

1- Firawn
2- True
3- Allah will help you now and in akhirah
4- Two
5- Quran
6- Excel in good

EPISODE - 32

1- Purify themselves
2- Strong
3- Honey
4- True
5- ——
6- InshaAllah

EPISODE - 33

1- It would run out
2- ——
3- No
4- Continuously
5- True
6- ——

EPISODE - 34

1- Healthy Mind
2- Just
3- True
4- ——
5- Scale
6- Shaitan - Poverty Allah - Forgiveness

EPISODE - 35

1- Hajar
2- A Prayer
3- Onion
4- 3 Quls
5- No
6- Yusuf

THE AZHARIS

ALSO IN THE SERIES:

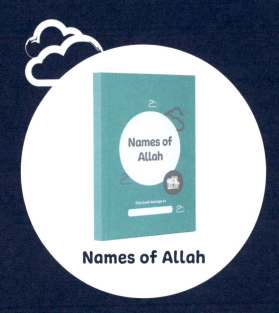

Names of Allah

**Juz by Juz
Stories**

www.theazharis.com

السَّلاَمُ عَلَيْكُمْ وَرَحْمَةُ اللهِ وَبَرَكَاتُهُ

InshaAllah we hope you have benefited from this series, that it brings us all closer to Allah and that He enables us to be amongst those in this hadith:

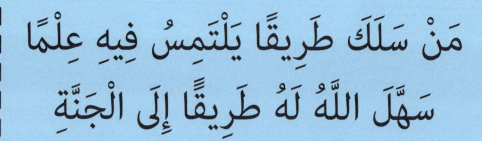

مَنْ سَلَكَ طَرِيقًا يَلْتَمِسُ فِيهِ عِلْمًا سَهَّلَ اللَّهُ لَهُ طَرِيقًا إِلَى الْجَنَّةِ

"Whoever takes a path upon which to obtain knowledge, Allah makes the path to Paradise easy for him."

- TIRMIDHI -

Sheikh Dr. Saalim Al-Azhari